MILITARY AIRCRAFT

F-35
LIGHTNING II

BY JOHN HAMILTON

VISIT US AT
WWW.ABDOPUBLISHING.COM

Published by ABDO Publishing Company, PO Box 398166, Minneapolis, MN 55439.
Copyright ©2012 by Abdo Consulting Group, Inc. International copyrights reserved in all
countries. No part of this book may be reproduced in any form without written permission
from the publisher. A&D Xtreme™ is a trademark and logo of ABDO Publishing Company.

Printed in the United States of America, North Mankato, Minnesota.
112011
012012

 PRINTED ON RECYCLED PAPER

Editor: Sue Hamilton
Graphic Design: Sue Hamilton
Cover Design: John Hamilton
Cover Photo: Department of Defense
Interior Photos: Corbis-pgs 24-25; Department of Defense-pgs 6-7 & 22; Joint Strike
Fighter Program-pgs 10-11, 12-13, 14-15 & 16-17; Lockheed Martin-pgs 1, 2-3, 4-5,
7 (inset), 8-9, 18-19, 23 (top & left bottom insets), 26-27, 30-31 & 32; United States
Air Force-pgs 20-21, United States Marine Corps-pg 23 (right bottom inset).

ABDO Booklinks
Web sites about Military Aircraft are featured on our Book Links pages. These links are
routinely monitored and updated to provide the most current information available. Web
site: www.abdopublishing.com

Library of Congress Cataloging-in-Publication Data

Hamilton, John, 1959-
    F-35 Lightning II / John Hamilton.
        p. cm. -- (Xtreme military aircraft)
    Includes index.
    ISBN 978-1-61783-269-7
    1. F-35 (Jet fighter plane)--Juvenile literature. I. Title.
    UG1242.F5H35565 2012
    623.74'64--dc23
                                    2011042334

TABLE OF CONTENTS

F-35 LIGHTNING II ★ ★ ★

The F-35 Lightning II is the United States military's next generation of fighter jet. It can fly many kinds of missions. It uses advanced technology. It also includes stealth construction. It is very hard for enemy forces to detect.

MISSIONS

The F-35 Lightning II
is a multirole fighter.
It can fly many kinds
of missions. It can fight
enemy planes (air-to-air).
It can attack ground targets
(air-to-ground). The F-35 can also
observe the enemy (reconnaissance)
and jam radar (electronic warfare).

The F-35 Lightning II is named in honor of the United States's P-38 Lightning and the United Kingdom's English Electric Lightning fighter aircraft.

An F-35 Lightning next to a U.S. P-38 Lightning.

ORIGINS

The United States started the Joint Strike Fighter program in the mid-1990s. Its goal was to replace several planes in America's aging fighter fleet. Manufacturer Lockheed Martin won the design competition with its X-35 prototype plane. Production began in 2001. The name of the plane was changed to the F-35 Lightning II.

The F-35 will eventually replace several planes. They include the F-16, A-10, F/A-18, AV-8B, the British Harrier GR7 and GR9, and the Canadian CF-18.

The first F-35 Lightning II (AF-01) leaves the runway near Lockheed Martin's Fort Worth, Texas, facility during its inaugural flight.

XTREME FACT

Final assembly of the F-35 will take place at Lockheed Martin's factory in Fort Worth, Texas.

THE F-35A

The F-35 has three versions. They have many common parts. This saves money. It also makes repairs easier.

An F-35A performs a test flight over the Grand Canyon, in Arizona.

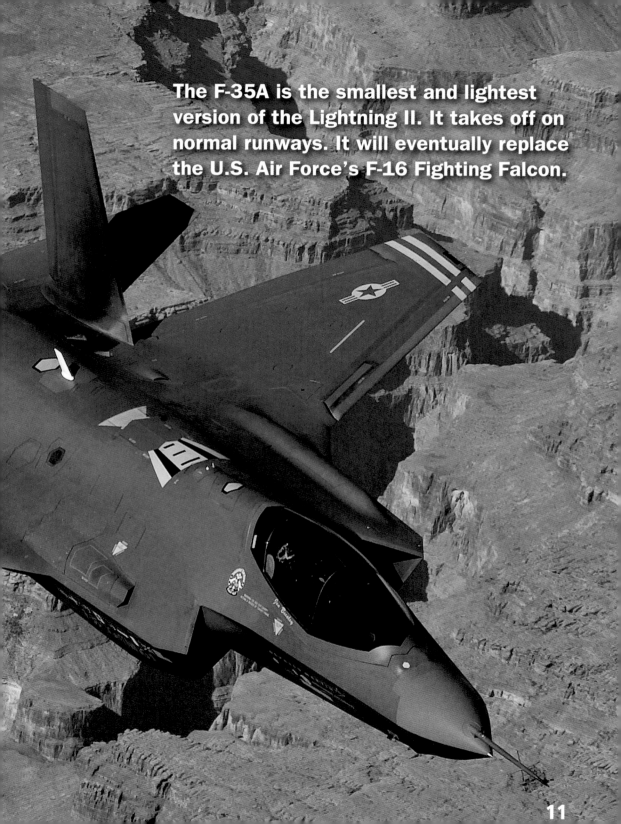

The F-35A is the smallest and lightest version of the Lightning II. It takes off on normal runways. It will eventually replace the U.S. Air Force's F-16 Fighting Falcon.

THE F-35B

The F-35B takes off and lands vertically. It is similar to the F-35A, but it has a smaller fuel tank. This makes room for its special engine. During takeoffs and landings, the engine thrust is directed downward. After takeoff, the plane returns to normal horizontal flight.

Aircraft that can land and take off vertically are useful on short runways or ships. The United States Marine Corps will be the main user of the F-35B. It will replace the Marine Corps's fleet of Harrier jets.

F-35Bs (above and below) practice vertical landings.

THE F-35C

The F-35C is the third version of the Lightning II.
It will be used by the United States Navy.
The F-35C has larger wings for easier takeoffs
and landings on aircraft carriers. The F-35C has
stronger landing gear.

The F-35C has a tailhook that grabs onto arresting cables on an aircraft carrier's flight deck when landing.

The F-35C is designed for use by the United States Navy.

F-35
LIGHTNING II
FAST FACTS

F-35A Lightning II Specifications

Function: Multirole attack and
                    fighter aircraft
Service Branch: U.S. Air Force, Marines,
                    and Navy
Manufacturer: Lockheed Martin
Crew: One

Length:	**51.1 feet (15.6 m)**
Height:	**15 feet (4.6 m)**
Wingspan:	**35 feet (10.7 m)**
Max Takeoff Weight:	**70,000 pounds (31,751 kg)**
Airspeed:	**Mach 1.6-plus**
	(1,200 mph/1,931 kph)
Ceiling:	**60,000 feet (18,288 m)**
Range:	**1,200 nautical miles**
	(1,381 miles, or 2,223 km)

STEALTH

It is very difficult for enemy forces to detect the F-35 Lightning II. The aircraft is made of material that absorbs radar waves. Its shape also makes it hard to detect.

An F-35 flies above the compass rose of Rogers Dry Lake at Edwards Air Force Base in California.

XTREME FACT

The F-35 Lightning II has a radar signature about the size of a metal golf ball.

ENGINE

The F-35 Lightning II has a single engine. It is a Pratt & Whitney F135. It is one of the most powerful engines ever used in a fighter jet. It has huge amounts of thrust. This gives the F-35 good turning ability. It also gives the F-35 the ability to carry many weapons.

The Pratt & Whitney F135 produces more than 43,000 pounds of thrust (191,274 Newtons).

A Pratt and Whitney F135 engine is tested before being installed in an F-35.

COCKPIT

WARNING - DO NOT CUT CANOPY WITHIN 3 INCHES OF CANOPY FRAME

WARNING - DO NOT CUT CANOPY WITHIN 3 INCHES OF CANOPY FRAME

The F-35 Lightning's cockpit has many electronic systems. They help pilots fly and fight the enemy. At the front of the cockpit is a large computer screen. It shows flight information and enemy targets.

Active Matrix Liquid Crystal Display image display

Sensor fusion

Binocular 40 degree by degree field-of-view

Integrated day and night camera

Ejection Safe to 600 knots equivalent air speed

F-35 pilots also use a helmet-mounted display. Pilots simply point their head at a target. The plane's computer locks onto the target and is then ready to shoot.

SENSORS

The F-35 Lightning II is filled with advanced electronics. They assist the pilot in the confusion of combat. The plane's sensors automatically recognize threats, such as enemy aircraft or missiles.

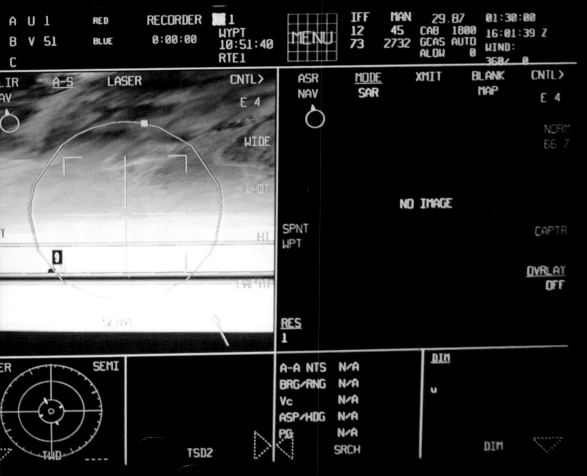

The F-35 Lightning can jam enemy radar. It can also share information with friendly aircraft.

WEAPONS

The F-35 Lightning II has two internal weapons bays. When missiles or bombs are ready to fire, the doors open. Otherwise, they stay closed to keep the F-35 stealthy.

The F-35 can also carry missiles and fuel tanks under its wings. It can fire air-to-air missiles (such as AIM-9X Sidewinder or AIM-132 ASRAAM missiles) and air-to-ground missiles (such as AGM-158 cruise missiles).

Missiles are shown in place on an F-35 cockpit screen.

XTREME FACT

The F-35A uses an internal GAU-12 Equalizer 25mm cannon for air-to-air combat and strafing enemy ground targets. The F-35B and F-35C use the cannon with an external gun mount.

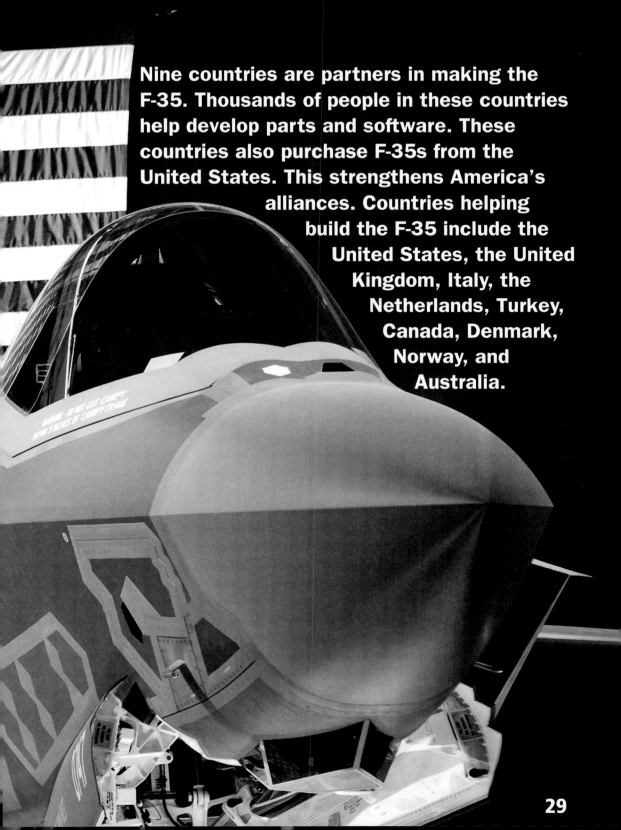

Nine countries are partners in making the F-35. Thousands of people in these countries help develop parts and software. These countries also purchase F-35s from the United States. This strengthens America's alliances. Countries helping build the F-35 include the United States, the United Kingdom, Italy, the Netherlands, Turkey, Canada, Denmark, Norway, and Australia.

GLOSSARY

Aircraft Carrier
A large warship that is a base for aircraft, which take off and land on its deck.

Mach
A common way to measure the speed of an aircraft when it approaches or exceeds the speed of sound in air. An aircraft traveling at Mach 1 is moving at the speed of sound, about 768 miles per hour (1,236 kph) when the air temperature is 68 degrees Fahrenheit (20 degrees C). An aircraft traveling at Mach 2 would be moving at twice the speed of sound.

Multirole
Able to perform more than one task or mission. The F-35 is a multirole aircraft. It can attack enemy targets in the air or on land.

Nautical Mile
A standard way to measure distance, especially when traveling in an aircraft or ship. It is based on the circumference of the Earth, the distance around the equator. This large circle is divided into

360 degrees. Each degree is further divided into 60 units called "minutes." A single minute of arc around the Earth is one nautical mile.

POUNDS OF THRUST

A way to measure the amount of force generated by aircraft engines (and other types of engines). The unit of measurement is usually in pounds (the metric equivalent is a unit called the Newton, named after the scientist Sir Isaac Newton). A pound of thrust is the amount of force needed to accelerate one pound of material 32 feet (9.8 m) per second every second (feet per second per second). One pound of thrust (32 feet per second per second) is the same as the acceleration of Earth's gravity.

RADAR

A way to detect objects, such as aircraft or ships, using electromagnetic (radio) waves. Radar waves are sent out by large dishes, or antennas, and then strike an object. The radar dish then detects the reflected wave, which can tell operators how big an object is, how fast it is moving, its altitude, and its direction. F-35s use modern stealth construction to minimize their radar reflection, making them very difficult for enemy forces to detect.

INDEX

For my mother, Gladys Millicent, who thought of
the idea, and my nephew, Jacob William, Cat Boy.

Clarion Books
a Houghton Mifflin Company imprint
215 Park Avenue South, New York, NY 10003
Text copyright © 1989 by Primrose Lockwood
Illustrations copyright © 1989 by Clara Vulliamy
All rights reserved.
For information about permission to reproduce
selections from this book, write to Permissions,
Houghton Mifflin Company, 2 Park Street, Boston, MA 02108.
Printed in Hong Kong

Lockwood, Primrose.
Cat boy! / by Primrose Lockwood : illustrations by Clara Vulliamy.
p.   cm.
Summary: Follows the adventures of a very young boy and his pet
cat throughout a typical day.
ISBN 0-395-55208-7
[1. Cats—Fiction.]   I. Vulliamy, Clara, ill.   II. Title.
PZ7.L819Cat   1990
[E]—dc20   90-35112
CIP
AC

Cat Boy!

Primrose Lockwood

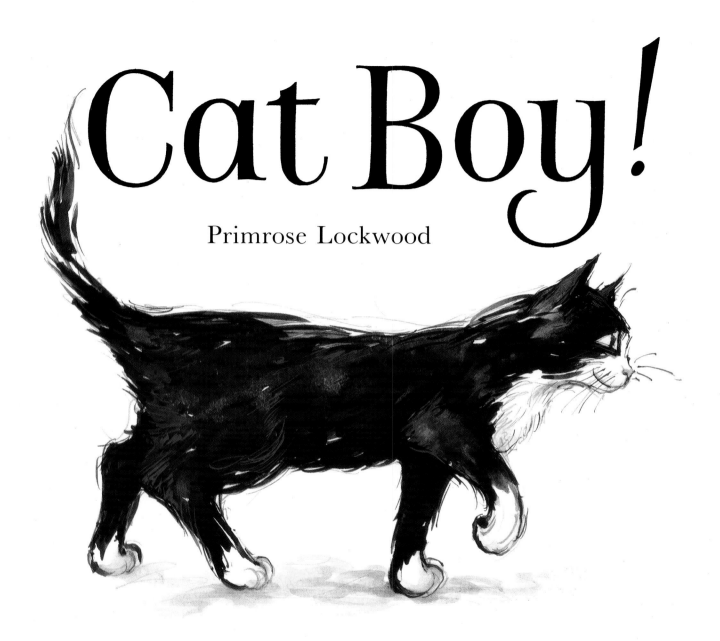

Pictures by Clara Vulliamy

CLARION BOOKS · NEW YORK

Boy waking,
Boy stretching,
Cat on his bed,
Cat boy!

Boy washing,
Boy dressing,
Cat at his feet,

Cat boy!

Boy eating,

Boy drinking,

Cat on his knee,

Cat boy!

Boy playing,

Boy climbing,
Cat following,

Cat boy!

Boy digging,

Boy hiding,

Cat watching,

Cat boy!

Boy helping,
Boy hammering,
Cat on his shoulders,
Cat boy!

Boy baking,
Boy mixing,
Cat purring,
Cat boy!

Boy shopping,

Boy buying,

Cat at the window,

Cat boy!

Boy drawing,
Boy painting,
Cat on the table,
Cat boy!

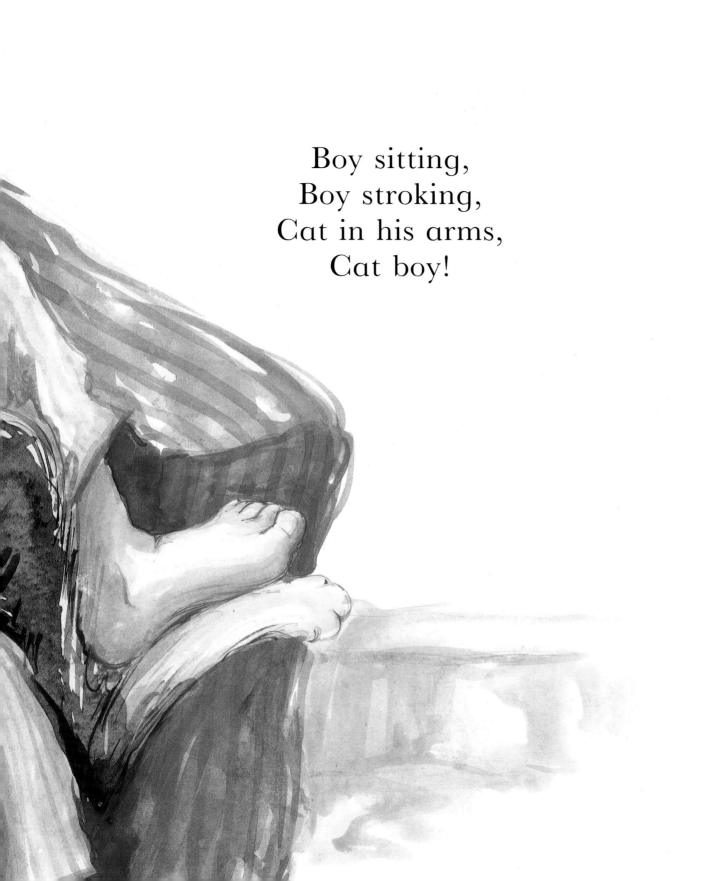

Boy sitting,
Boy stroking,
Cat in his arms,
Cat boy!

Boy reading,

Boy looking,

Cat on his book,

Cat boy!

Boy tiring,
Boy sleeping,
Cat on his bed,
Cat boy!